What's a Yiayia?

A BOOK ABOUT GRANDMOTHERS

Stella Stamatakis
Illustrated by Oscar Fa

Published in Australia by
Butter Fingers Books
ABN: 69 334 538 893
Email: stellastamatakis@me.com
Website: www.stellastamatakis.com

First published in Australia 2019
Copyright © Stella Stamatakis 2019

All rights reserved. No part of this publication may
be reproduced, stored in a retrieval system, or transmitted,
in any form or by any means without the prior written
permission of the publisher, nor be otherwise circulated
in any form of binding or cover other than that in which
it is published and without a similar condition being
imposed on the subsequent purchaser.

National Library of Australia Cataloguing–in–Publication entry

Creator: Stamatakis, Stella, author.
TITLE: What's a Yiayia
ISBN: 978-0-6482367-0-2 (paperback)
ISBN: 978-0-6482367-1-9 (hardback)
ISBN: 978-0-6482367-2-6 (epub)

Target Audience: For children aged 4-9
Subjects: Multiculturalism - Juvenile fiction.
Cultural diversity - Juvenile fiction. Acceptance - Children's stories
Other Creators / Contributors: Fa, Oscar, illustrator

Cover layout, illustrations and design by Oscar Fa
Printed by Ingram Spark

Disclaimer
All care has been taken in the preparation of the information
herein, but no responsibility can be accepted by the publisher
or author for any damages resulting from the misinterpretation
of this work. All contact details given in this book were current
at the time of publication, but are subject to change.

 A catalogue record for this book is available from the National Library of Australia

For all grandmothers throughout the world, whatever you may be named. Thank you. SS

Eleni simply adored Mondays. It was her favourite day of the week, as this was the day her Yiayia picked her up from school. Eleni sat in the circle at group time, and she couldn't wait to share her exciting news.

Show and Share

"I'm going to my Yiayia Anna's tonight!" she exclaimed.
Luca looked at her confused. "What's a Yiayia?" he asked.

"My grandma, of course!" Eleni replied.
"She comes from Greece."

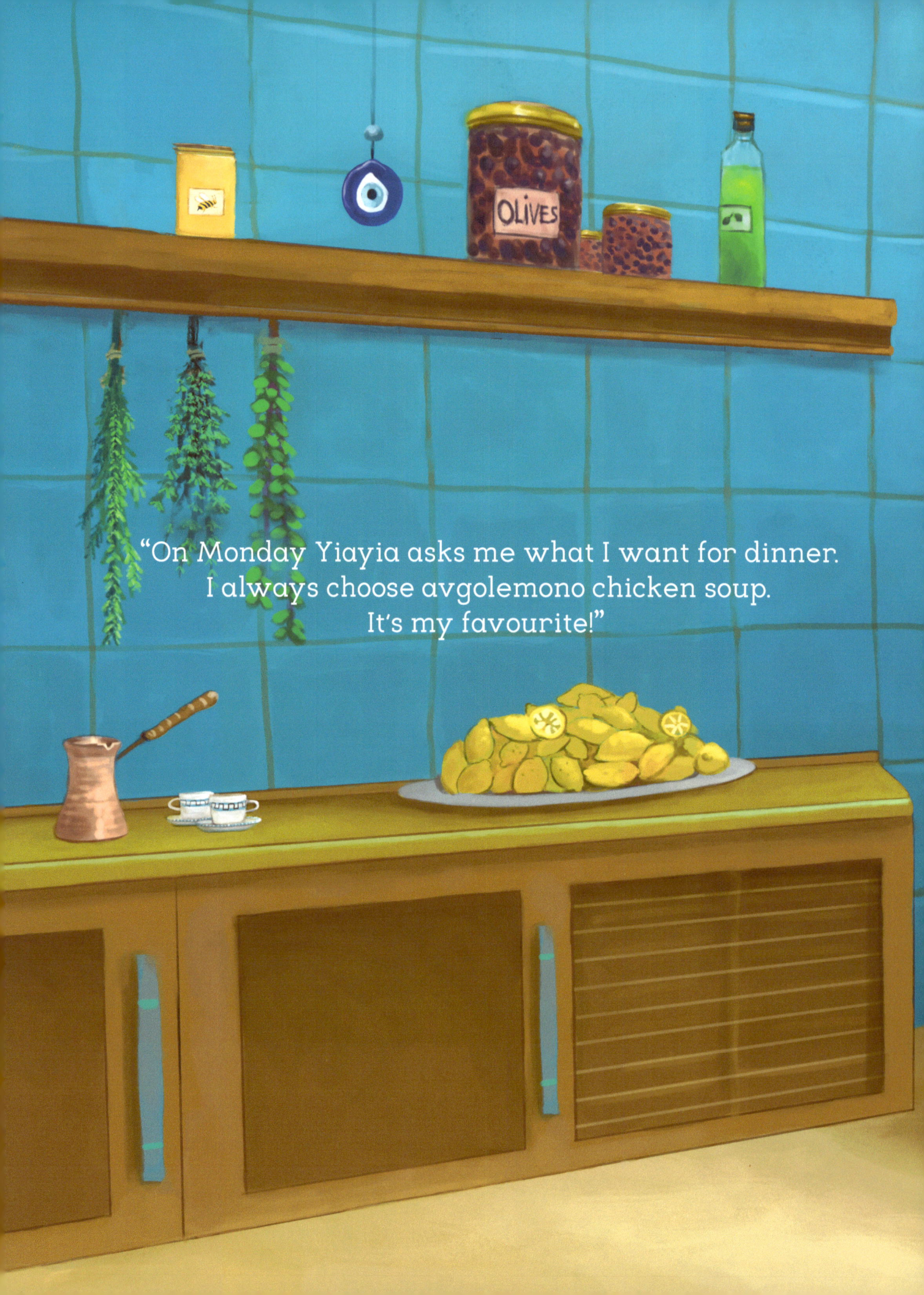

"We boil the chicken, juice the lemon and I even get to beat the egg whites until they're frothy. When it's ready we sit together, laugh and eat. It's really delicious."

Luca smiled and nodded his head. "I call my grandma Nonna Maria. She comes from Italy and makes the best pasta in the world."

"When we're together on Tuesdays we make ravioli. I help my nonna cut out the little squares of pasta with her special zig zag cutter," Luca grinned.

"It's so much fun! We boil the ravioli, toss it through the Napoli sauce and gobble it up. I love cooking and eating with Nonna, especially when she hugs me tight."

Rubi joined in, and told them about her Nanna Mavis, who was born in Shepparton. "My nanna is the most awesome baker in the world," declared Rubi.

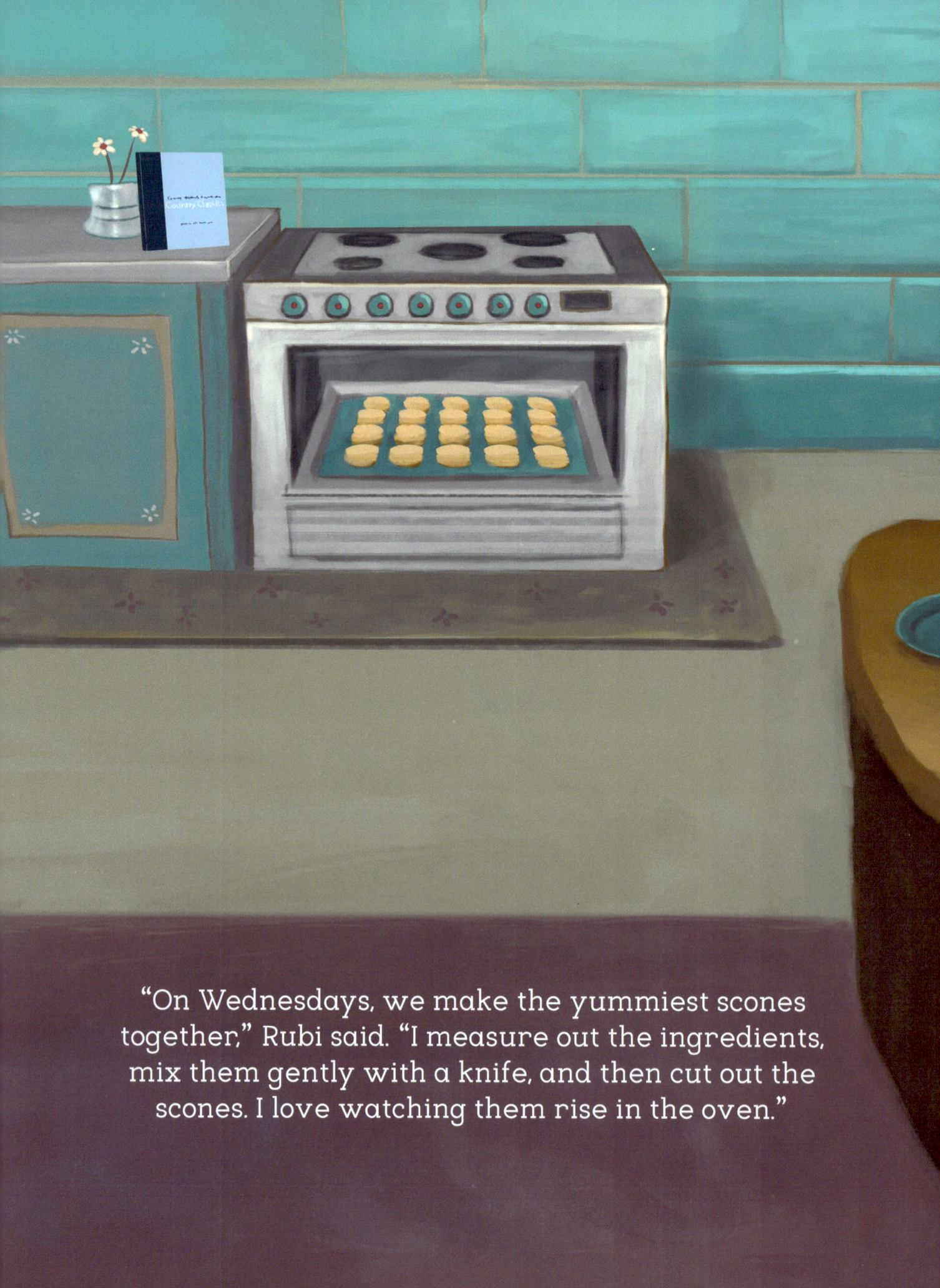

"On Wednesdays, we make the yummiest scones together," Rubi said. "I measure out the ingredients, mix them gently with a knife, and then cut out the scones. I love watching them rise in the oven."

"We beat the cream, set the table and share afternoon tea." Rubi patted her tummy. "I love eating them with my nanna, it's so much fun being with her."

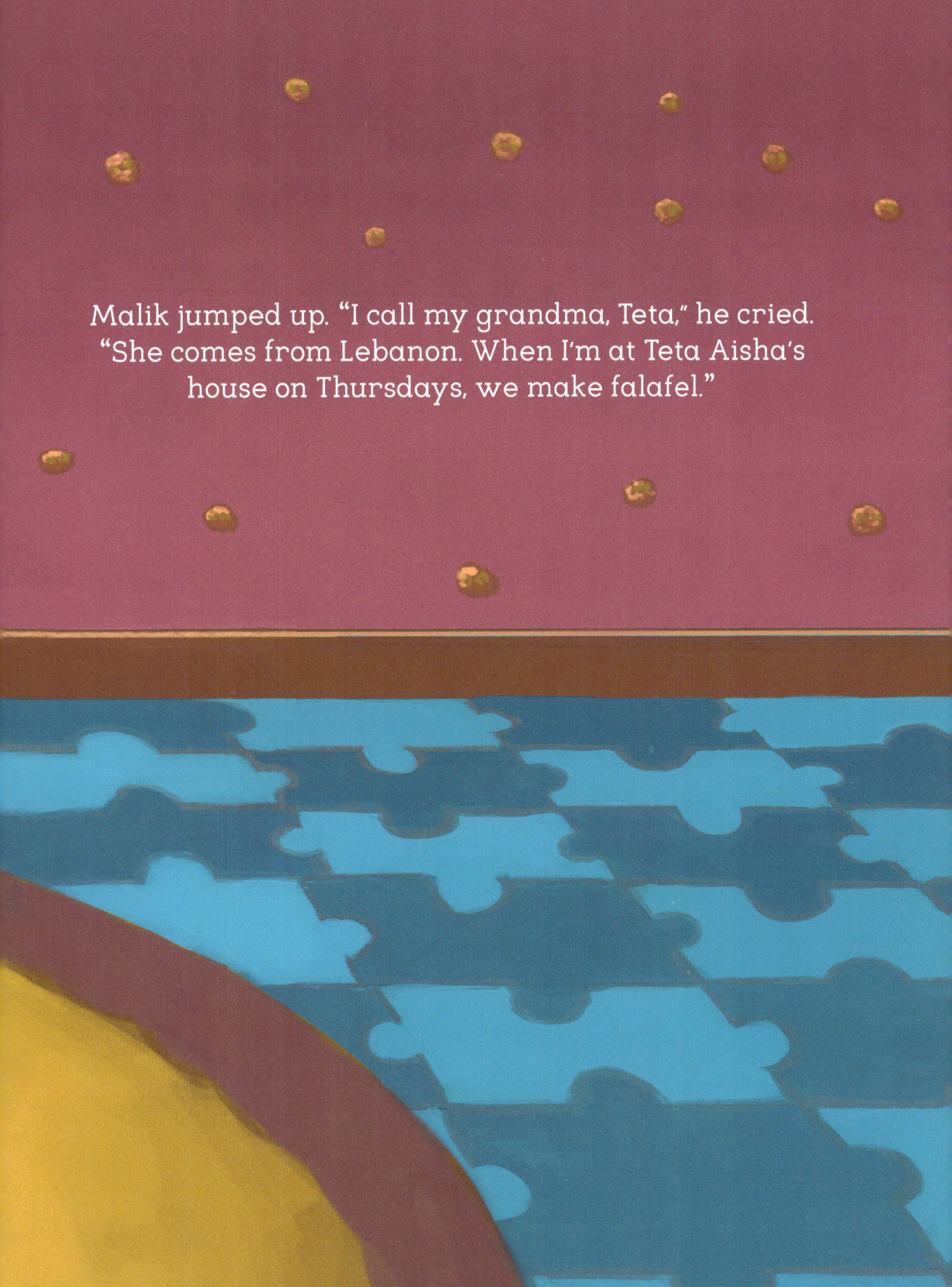

Malik jumped up. "I call my grandma, Teta," he cried. "She comes from Lebanon. When I'm at Teta Aisha's house on Thursdays, we make falafel."

"The balls of bright green mixture feel so squishy between my fingers," Malik said. "I make some big ones, some small ones, and sometimes they are even the same size as my teta's."

Malik cupped his hands into a perfect circle.
"I love eating and spending time with Teta.
She makes me feel so warm inside!"

Kim smiled at her friends.
"My grandma is called Ba," she announced.
"My Ba Tam is from Vietnam. Every Friday we make rice paper rolls together."

"Dipping the rice paper in water is tricky so I have to be quick. When the skin is soft, I add the mixture and roll it." Kim grinned widely.

"Ba and I make enough for all the family.
The best part is eating together.
It makes my heart sing."

By now, Adelina was getting very hungry, and she licked her lips loudly. Everyone in the class looked at her. "I call my grandma, Abuela," she exclaimed. "She comes from Spain."

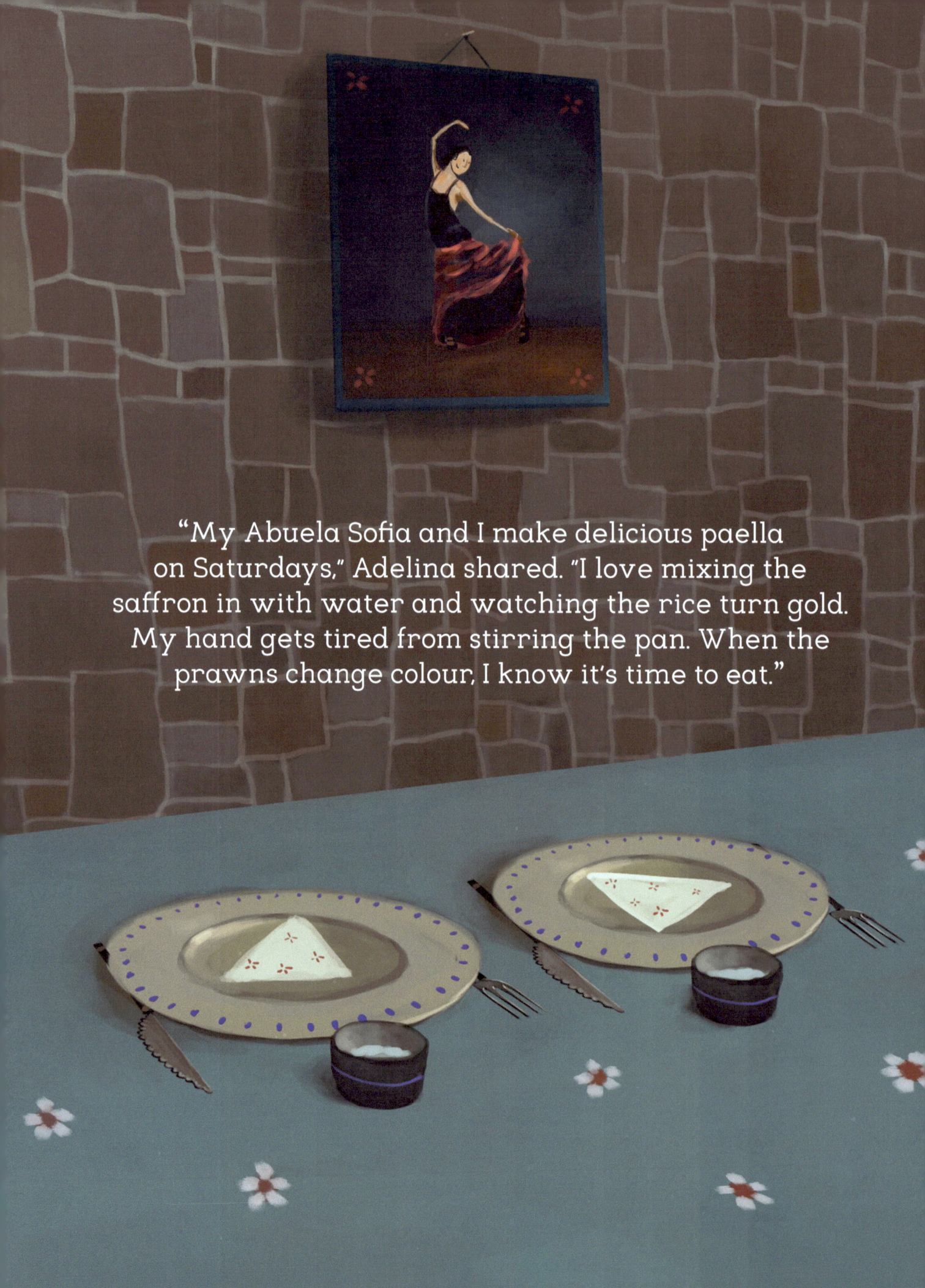

"My Abuela Sofia and I make delicious paella on Saturdays," Adelina shared. "I love mixing the saffron in with water and watching the rice turn gold. My hand gets tired from stirring the pan. When the prawns change colour, I know it's time to eat."

"Abuela and I sit together with the pan in the middle of the table. There's always plenty for everyone."

Lily was fascinated by all she'd heard
"I call my grandma Nainai," she said.
"My Nainai Lin comes all the way from China."

"On Sundays when I visit her, we make dumplings and have yum cha together. I roll out the pastry with my own tiny rolling pin," said Lily proudly.

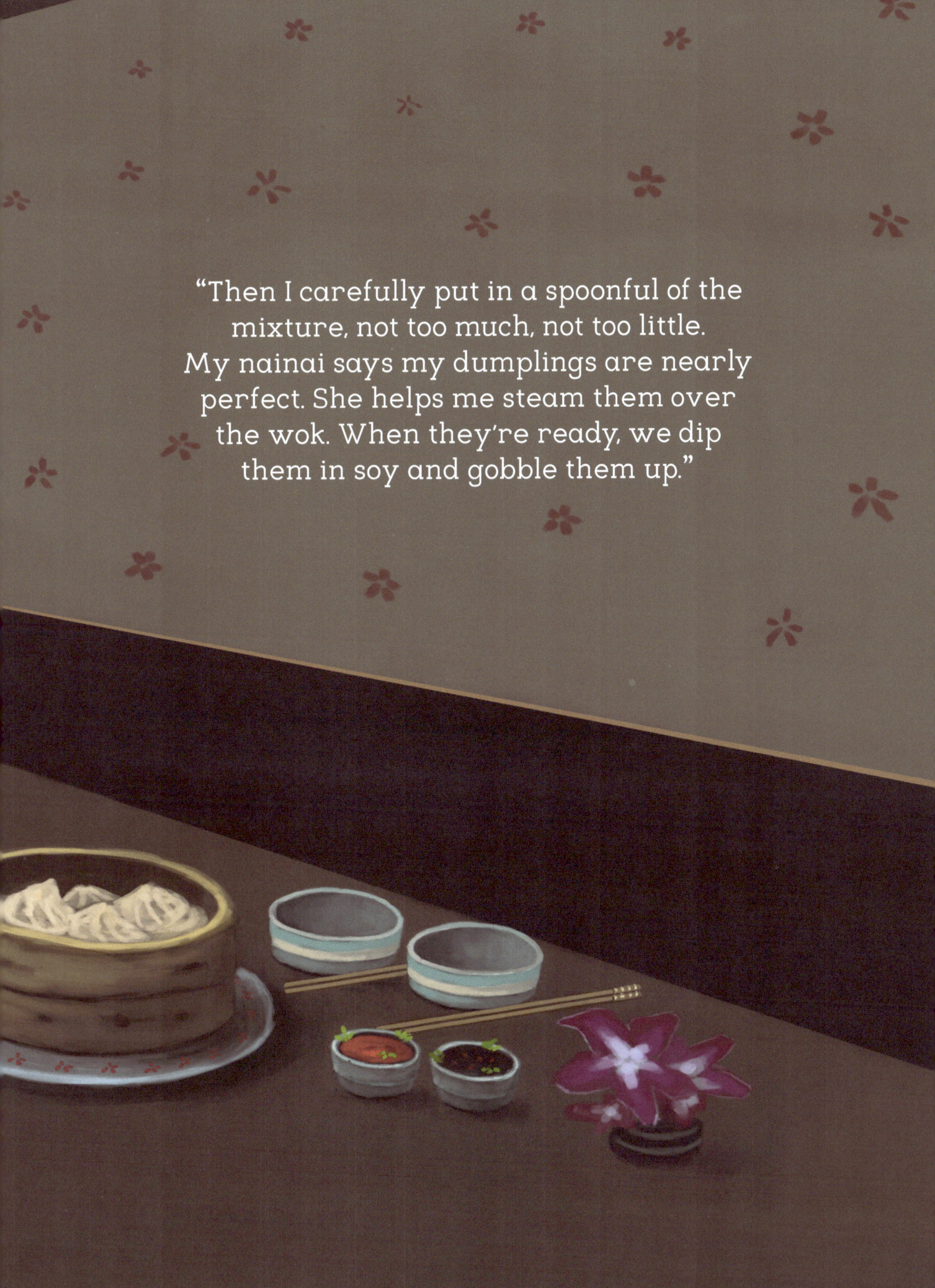

"Then I carefully put in a spoonful of the mixture, not too much, not too little. My nainai says my dumplings are nearly perfect. She helps me steam them over the wok. When they're ready, we dip them in soy and gobble them up."

Eleni smiled and looked around at all her classmates. "We're all the same, and just a little bit different too. Isn't that wonderful. We all love our yiayia's and they love us."

What's a Yiayia?

About the Author

Stella Stamatakis is a primary school teacher of over 20 years. She loves telling stories, travelling and helping others. She's loud, funny and adores making mischief, having fun and eating. Stella lives with her husband Frank, their two children, Elle and Max, and dog, Luna.

About the Illustrator

Oscar is a freelance French artist specialising in concept art and digital illustration. He undertakes projects such as cover designs, illustrating fiction and children's picture books. He has always been curious and passionate about painting, and tries to fill his days with colour!

www.ingramcontent.com/pod-product-compliance
Lightning Source LLC
Chambersburg PA
CBHW042143290426
44110CB00002B/95